AN ESSAY

ON

APPARITIONS,

IN WHICH

THEIR APPEARANCE IS ACCOUNTED FOR

BY CAUSES WHOLLY INDEPENDENT OF

Preternatural Agency.

BY

JOHN ALDERSON, M.D.

SENIOR PHYSICIAN TO THE HULL GENERAL INFIRMARY; CONSULTING PHYSICIAN TO THE LYING-IN CHARITY; PRESIDENT OF THE HULL LITERARY AND PHILOSOPHICAL SOCIETY; HONORARY MEMBER OF THE YORKSHIRE PHILOSOPHICAL SOCIETY; CORRESPONDING MEMBER OF THE MEDICO-CHIRURGICAL SOCIETY, EDINBURGH, &c. &c. &c.

Ea quæ rerum simulacra vocamus.—LUCRETIUS.

TO

Sir JAMES M'GRIGOR, M.D.F.R.S.

DIRECTOR-GENERAL,

ARMY MEDICAL DEPARTMENT,

&c. &c. &c.

IN TESTIMONY OF

THE HIGH ESTEEM IN WHICH HE HOLDS HIS

TALENTS

AND PROFESSIONAL ACQUIREMENTS,

THIS ESSAY

IS RESPECTFULLY INSCRIBED,

BY

THE AUTHOR.

INTRODUCTION.

The following Essay was written originally for a Literary Society, to prove the reality of Ghosts, and by accounting for their appearance from natural causes, to remove those impressions of terror which are made upon the minds of youth, when apparitions are supposed to be preternatural.

This subject was illustrated by a number of cases, drawn from the author's own experience, and which cases were all of them capable of being authenticated at the time by the members of the society.

It was read in manuscript for several years afterwards, in different places, and was published, unknown to the author, in the Edinburgh Medical and Chirurgical Journal, in the year 1810.

From the notice which his peculiar hypothesis obtained at the time, the author was led to believe it had drawn the attention of the public, and he reprinted it in 1811 with some necessary corrections, and added it to a fourth edition of his Essay on the Rhus Toxicodendron, then in the press. In 1813, an eminent and learned physician at Manchester published as new the same theory, supported by ancient history and traditional stories, which, if not equivocal, could not be so well authenticated as those to be found in the following essay.

As no notice whatever was taken of his publication, the author has been induced, at the recommendation of his friends, to republish it in a more book-like form, not only to prevent all suspicion of plagiarism, but to assert his claim, and show his right to whatever novelty or merit there may be in the theory itself.*

He thinks himself fully entitled to adopt or take to himself the concluding paragraph of the " Essay towards a new Theory of Apparitions."

" By the key *I* have furnished, the reader of history is released from the embarrassment of rejecting evidence in

---

* A truly ingenious and elegant writer has done the author ample justice, by allowing his claim to a priority of publication. Vide Shakspeare and his Times; by Nathan Drake, M. D.

some of the plainest narratives, or of experiencing uneasy doubts, when the solution might be rendered perfectly simple." Vide Essay by I. Ferriar, M.D.

CONTENTS.

CHAP. I.

Universal belief in Ghosts. — Addison; his Opinions. — Luther; his Ideas of Madmen, and of Idiots, - - - - - - - 13

CHAP. II.

Statement of facts upon which the Hypothesis is meant to be founded. — Cases. — Treatment and Cure, - - - - - - 20

CHAP. III.

Hallucination distinguished from Partial Insanity, from Delirium, from Somnambulism, from Reverie. — Mahomet. — Jacob Behmen, and other Visionaries, - 40

CHAP. IV.

Locke; his Opinions. — Shakspeare — Macbeth — Hamlet. — Conclusion, - 47

CHAPTER I.

UNIVERSAL BELIEF IN GHOSTS. — ADDISON; HIS OPINIONS. — LUTHER; HIS IDEAS OF MADMEN AND IDIOTS.

"What all the world says must be true," is an old adage; and, as old sayings have their foundation in the experience of ages, I am disposed to believe them true. Now it is a general observation, amounting to an established fact, that in all countries whose history we have long been acquainted with, as well as in those to which the active and enterprising spirit of modern discovery has penetrated, there has constantly been found a belief in apparitions. This general notion or faith of the re-appearance of those who have departed this life, could not, in all cases, have arisen from the transmission of the poetic inventions of former times; because countries have been discovered, where we cannot suppose, or at least cannot trace, any previous race of men, of superior intelligence, capable, like Homer or Ossian, of transmitting the records of antiquity; and, with regard to the intervention of super natural agency, in communicating or revealing knowledge to men, it behoves us, I think, to keep in mind an old maxim, "*Nec Deus intersit nisi dignus vindice nodus:*" Let us take care never to introduce the miraculous agency of Providence to account for effects, where common agents by natural causes can be found. Nor ought we hastily to abandon our inquiries after such second causes, merely because we may be told that they are mysteries. At the same time, we have much cause to be thankful to the Almighty Governor of all things, when such circumstances and events dispose the wicked to turn from the error of their ways, as in the case of Colonel Gardiner; or when they tend to strengthen and encourage the good in the way of welldoing, as in the instance of the truly respected, the Reverend Vincent Perronet.*

* The remarkable conversion of Colonel Gardiner, by an apparition, is sufficiently well known. The history of Mr. Perronet † requires further

† He was the grandfather and instructor of my inestimable friend, the late Mrs. Thompson, who imbibed, under his tuition, those Christian principles, which she unremittingly exemplified in practice during life. In the discharge of one of these duties, she accompanied her lovely and beloved daughter to Penzance, in search of that health for her which had been despaired of at home. She was prevented, by premature death, in an apoplectic fit, from witnessing the last distressing scene: — her daughter outlived her but a short time. They were buried in the same vault at the Land's End,

" Where they alike in pious hope repose."

The re-appearance of departed spirits, however, is generally attributed to the

---

notice. He was upwards of fifty years vicar of Shoreham, in Kent, was a very amiable man, and a popular preacher.

He seems to have considered himself as especially called, from his earliest years, to the study of the Scriptures, with a view of preaching the " true gospel of Christ." He had several " spiritual experiences," through the medium of apparitions, which made a lasting impression on his mind, though not attended with any " fright or terror."

When he was an infant, about four years of age, he was waked in the night by something lying on his forehead, which felt like the impression of a very cold hand. It continued some time after he was awake, when he perceived a tall man close to the bed-side, who looked very sternly at him.

Much about this time he saw another person standing on the opposite side of the bed, dressed in very mean apparel, whose aspect seemed earnest, serious, and composed. However, what the design of either of these appearances might be, he pretends not to know. When he was between five and six years old, being on a visit to some of his father's relations in Switzerland, he was travelling concealment of some trifling treasure, or because the rites and fees of sepulture have not been duly paid.

" But if the flinty prison of the grave
Could loose its doors, and let the spirit flee;
Why not return the wise, the just, the brave,
And set once more the pride of ages free?"

---

over some high mountains on horseback, but through the neglect of the guide, who had the care of his horse, instead of pursuing the proper road, the horse directed his course towards a large lake; but before he entered, he saw very plainly one like a man, in a white garment, coming upon the water towards him: upon which the horse turned away, and got into the right road again. The first step he had taken into the lake, both the horse and the rider must have been inevitably lost, as he was afterwards informed.

One night in particular, when he was broad awake, he heard a variety of disagreeable voices, and felt several blows from invisible hands; so that he might literally have said, " The messengers of Satan were sent to buffet him."

I need only quote the authority of one of our most approved writers, without referring to a tribe of authors, for the proof of the universality of this belief.

"I think," says Addison, "a person who is terrified with the imagination of ghosts and spectres, much more reasonable than one, who, contrary to the reports of all historians, sacred and profane, ancient and modern, and to the traditions of all nations, thinks the appearance of ghosts fabulous and groundless. Could not I give myself up to this general testimony of mankind, I should to the relations of particular persons, who are now living, and whom I cannot distrust in other matters of fact." In the paragraph which I have now quoted, you have not only a record of history, as to the universality of the belief, but the candid confession of a man of the first talents, that he firmly believed in ghosts and apparitions, though he has not favoured us with any theory respecting their origin.

Is it not mortifying to know that such a man as Luther was a firm believer in apparitions as supernatural agents; and that he should suppose madmen and idiots to be possessed by evil spirits; nay, that he should actually have quarrelled with the physicians, who attributed these affections to natural causes?

CHAPTER II.

STATEMENT OF FACTS UPON WHICH THE HYPOTHESIS IS MEANT TO BE FOUNDED. — CASES. — TREATMENT AND CURE.

In the investigation of any subject, it is generally the best method to begin by a statement of the facts upon which the hypothesis is meant to be founded. I shall, therefore, in this chapter, present some cases for the consideration of my readers, which will, in my opinion, strongly tend to account for the universality of the notion mentioned in the preceding chapter; for they will prove, that the belief in apparitions, ghosts, and spectres, is not only well founded, but that these appearances are perfectly natural, arising from secondary physical causes, and depending on circumstances to which all nations, all mankind, are equally liable; and therefore a general concurrence of opinion on these points must be as universal as the principle of population itself.

CASE I.

I was called upon some time ago to visit Mr. ———, who at that time kept a dram shop. Having at different times attended him, and thence knowing him very well, I was struck with something singular in his manner on my first entrance. He went up stairs with me, but evidently hesitated, occasionally, as he went. When he got into his chamber, he expressed some apprehension, lest I should consider him insane, and send him to the asylum at York, whither I had not long before sent one of his pot-companions.—" Whence all these apprehensions?—What is the matter with you?—Why do you look so full of terror?" He then sat down, and gave me a history of his complaint.

About a week or ten days before, after drawing some liquor in his cellar for a girl, he desired her to take away the oysters which lay upon the floor, and which he supposed she had dropped;—the girl, thinking him drunk, laughed at him, and went out of the room.—He endeavoured to take them up himself, and to his great astonishment could find none. — He was met going out of the cellar, when at the door he met a soldier, whose looks he did not like, attempting to enter.

He desired to know what he wanted there; and upon receiving no answer, but, as he thought, a menacing look, he sprang forward to seize the intruder, and, to his no small surprise, found that it was a phantom. The cold sweat hung upon his brow— he trembled in every limb — it was the dusk of the evening; as he walked along the passage the phantom flitted before his eyes — he attempted to follow it, resolutely determined to satisfy himself; but as this vanished, there appeared others at a distance, and he exhausted himself by fruitless attempts to lay hold of them. He hastened to his family, with marks of terror and confusion; for, though a man hitherto of the most undaunted resolution, he confessed to me that he now felt what it was to be completely terrified. During the whole of that night he was constantly tormented with a variety of spectres, sometimes of people who had been long dead, at other times of friends who were living; and harassed himself with continually getting out of bed, to ascertain whether the people he saw were real or not. Nor could he always distinguish who were and who were not real customers, when they came into the room, so that his conduct became the subject of observation; and though it was for a time attributed to private drinking, it was at last suspected to arise from some other cause. When I was sent for, the family were under the full conviction that he was insane, although they confessed, that in every thing, except the foolish notion of seeing apparitions, he was perfectly rational and steady. During the whole of the time that he was relating his case to me, and his mind was fully occupied, he felt the most gratifying relief, for in all that time he had not seen one apparition; and he was elated with pleasure indeed, when I told him I should not send him to the asylum, since his was a complaint I could cure at his own house. But whilst I was writing a prescription, and had suffered him to be at rest, I saw him get up suddenly, and go with a hurried step to the door.—"What did you do that for?"—he looked ashamed and mortified, and replied, "I had been so well whilst in conversation with you, that I could not believe that the phantom I saw enter the room was not really a soldier, and I got up to convince myself."

I need not here detail particularly the medical treatment adopted; but it may be as well to state the circumstances which probably led to the complaint, and the principle acted on in the cure. Some time previously he had had a quarrel with a drunken soldier, who attempted, against his inclination, to enter his house at an unseasonable hour, and in the struggle to turn him out, the soldier drew his bayonet, and, having struck him across the temples, divided the temporal artery; in consequence of which he lost a very large quantity of blood before a surgeon arrived, there being no one present who knew that, in such cases, simple compression with the finger upon the spouting artery, would stop the effusion of blood. He had scarcely recovered from the effects of this loss of blood, when he undertook to accompany a friend in his walking-match against time, in which he went forty-two miles in nine hours. Elated with success, he spent the whole of the following day in drinking; but found himself, a short time afterwards, so much out of health, that he came to the resolution of abstaining altogether from liquor. It was in the course of the week following this abstinence from his usual habits, that he had the disease he now complained of. All his symptoms continued to increase for several days till I saw him, allowing him no time for rest. Never was he able to get rid of these shadows by night when in bed, nor by day when in motion; though he sometimes walked miles with that view, and at others went into a variety of company. He told me he suffered even bodily pain, from the severe lashing of a waggoner with his whip, who came every night to a particular corner of his room, but who always disappeared when he jumped out of bed to retort, which he did several nights successively. The whole of this complaint was effectually removed by bleeding, by leeches, and by active purgatives. After the first employment of these means, he saw no more phantoms in the day time; and after the second, once only, between sleeping and waking, saw the milkman in his bedroom. He has remained perfectly rational and well ever since, and can go out in the dark as fearlessly as ever, being fully convinced that the ghosts which he was so confident he saw, were merely the creatures of disease.

CASE II.

I was soon after called to visit Mrs. B., a fine old lady, about 80 years of age, whom

I had frequently visited in fits of the gout. She was seized with an unusual deafness, and with great distension of the organs of digestion, at a period, when, from her general feelings, she expected the gout. From this time she was visited by the phantoms of some of her friends, whom she had not invited, and whom she at first so far considered as actually present, that she told them she was very sorry she could not hear them speak, nor keep up the conversation with them, she would therefore order the card table; and she rang the bell for that purpose. Upon the entrance of the servant, the whole party disappeared—she could not help expressing her surprise to her maid that they should all go away so abruptly; and could scarcely believe her when she affirmed there had been nobody in the room. She was so ashamed, when convinced of the deception under which she laboured, that she suffered, without complaining, for many days and nights together, the intrusion of a variety of phantoms; and had some of her finest feelings wrought upon by the exhibition of friends long lost, who only came to cheat her fancy, and revive sensations that time had almost obliterated. Having determined not again to mention the subject, she contented herself with merely ringing her bell, finding she could always get rid of the phantoms by the entrance of her maid, whenever they became distressing. It was not till some time after she had thus suffered, that she could bring herself to relate her distress to me. She was all this time convinced of her own rationality, and so were those friends who really visited her; for they never could find any one circumstance in her conduct and conversation, to lead them to suspect her being in the smallest degree deranged, though unwell. This complaint was entirely removed by cataplasms to the feet, and gentle purgatives; and terminated, a short time afterwards, in a slight fit of the gout. She remained to the end of her life, in the perfect enjoyment of her health and faculties.

CASE III.

About the same period I visited Mr. R., who was seized on his passage from America with a most excruciating headache. He obtained some temporary relief from the formation of matter under the scalp; but swellings came on in the throat, and he had some difficulty of respiration when in bed. At this time he complained to me that he had troublesome dreams, and that he seemed to dream whilst awake. In a short time after this, he told me he had, for an hour or two, been convinced that he had seen his wife and family, when his right judgment told him that they were in America; a few nights afterwards, the impression was so strong, and the conversation he had with his son so very particular and important, that he could not help relating the whole to his friends in the morning, requesting to know if his wife and son were not actually arrived from America, and at that time in the house. I was sent for to hold a consultation with his friends, respecting the state of his mind. He evidently felt that they all took him to be insane. As soon as I entered the room, he asked me if the disease he then laboured under could produce the imagination of spectres and apparitions. He had been hitherto, he said, an unbeliever in ghosts, but had certainly been tormented by spectres during the night, when perfectly awake. He felt himself sane, and his friends all acknowledged, that, in every thing else, he was as sound in mind as ever he was in his life. Having explained to him the nature and extent of his complaint, and having assured him, that these visionary appearances would cease with his bodily sufferings, he and his friends were rendered easy in their minds. As the disease, however, still continued, the phantoms became afterwards more troublesome, so that he could not bear to go into his bed-room, where every picture was associated with them, conjuring up the spirits of the departed, and introducing a train of unpleasant companions. He remained after this in a low room, and was for a time free from intruders; but in a bright brass lock again seeing his transatlantic friends, never afterwards could he look towards it without the same illusion; and when I have been with him, and have purposely taken up a book, I have seen him hold conversation in his mind's eye with them; I have even known him momentarily consider me as hearing and seeing them too —I say momentarily, for he was a man of strong parts, and perfectly convinced of the nature of the complaint; therefore, whenever I spoke, and he turned from the lock, he could converse on religion, physic, and politics, as well as ever. He then changed his house; the matter again formed under his scalp, and he is now in a state of convalescence, and totally free from such visitations.

These people were all well at the time this essay was first read to the society for which it was originally written, and were as capable as I am of relating all these circumstances: they were convinced that these were only phantoms, that had no connection whatever with the persons they represented; and that their existence was only in their own disordered imaginations. But I am persuaded, that had the diseases under which they laboured gone off after the first appearance of the phantoms, or had they been thus attacked in the night only, — so terrified, so astonished, so convinced were they of their reality, (as ghosts I mean,) that no power on earth would ever have altered that opinion: nor could any one have satisfied them that it was a disease under which they themselves laboured; so that they would have passed through life with the full persuasion of having seen a ghost, in the common acceptation of the term. The long continuance of the complaint, the opportunities afforded, both by day and night, of ascertaining the nature of the appearances, and the full conviction produced from their entire expulsion by remedies, without any delusion, or mystycism, or magic, dispelled every idea of their supernatural origin, and they no more believed in the common notion of ghosts than I do. *

* As it has only been my object to account for such apparitions as are here related, I have been at no pains to explain the various delusions of the mischievous who have gone about to frighten their neighbours, like the Cock-lane ghost and others; nor those appearances which have been produced,

CASE IV.

I some time ago received the following letter, in which the patient gives a full account of his own case: —

" I am oppressed by a complaint the most extraordinary I ever heard of; it only afflicted me this morning, and has occasionally shown itself during the day. My only complaint is that which generally accompanies a series of hard living; I can eat tolerably well, but I had a most violent bilious attack the latter end of

---

sometimes purposely, sometimes accidentally, and which depend on mechanical and optical deceptions; such as the reflection of persons passing strong lights on a hill at a small distance, seen obliquely on the church windows, and which has the appearance of ghosts flitting within the church. They are all as easily explained as those I have mentioned; but they have been explained by others, and form no part of my plan.

last week, and vomited incessantly. This morning I awoke early, after two very unusually sleepless nights, and to my surprise I saw horrid and ghastly spectres constantly present to my imagination; but to my greatest surprise, during a walk in my grounds, about eleven o'clock, I fancied I saw a set of poachers on my estate, coursing a hare. I followed them on foot for several miles, they being present to my view all the time.

" As they were on horseback, they eluded my pursuit. Having returned to my house, I again saw them, a short time afterwards, similarly occupied in the front of my house: I immediately ordered my horse, and again pursued them for miles, until, on taking a large fence, I suddenly lost all sight of them, and I am now fully convinced that the whole was an illusion. In my family affairs and business I am competent, but very uncomfortable, fearing it may affect my intellect. I therefore hope to see you here as soon as possible this evening. I forgot to say, that, when not very sober, I had a fall from my horse a few days ago, but did not receive any material injury at the time."

CHAP. III.

HALLUCINATION DISTINGUISHED FROM PARTIAL INSANITY, FROM DELIRIUM, FROM SOMNAMBULISM, FROM REVERIE. — MAHOMET. — JACOB BEHMEN, AND OTHER VISIONARIES.

Having made out the universality of the belief in ghosts, I trust that I have also not only established the reality of such appearances, but demonstrating, from physical causes, how this notion has arisen, have satisfactorily proved, that the cause lies, not in the perturbed spirits of the departed, but in the disordered functions of the living.

The hallucination, which the foregoing cases detail, may be distinguished from

ON APPARITIONS. 41

partial insanity, from delirium, from somnambulism, and from reverie, to all of which it bears some resemblance. In partial insanity, the patient, though sensible on most subjects, is generally intent on one particular train of thought; and, whenever he has occasion to speak upon that subject, he flies off into some absurd notion or other, and no argument whatever can drive him from his purpose. In delirium, the patient neither knows where he is nor what he does, except for a few moments, when violently roused. In somnambulism, there are certain voluntary motions performed, without our being sensible of volition. In reverie, the mind is so wholly intent on its own particular train of thoughts, that the patient takes no notice whatever of any thing around him.

But in such cases as I have detailed, there is no point on which the patients can be said to be irrational; they merely state that they perceive objects, where we know, and where they can very easily convince themselves, that they do not exist:—

> ——— " their thoughts
> Are combinations of disjointed things;
> And forms impalpable and unperceived
> Of others' sight, familiar are to them."

When this circumstance occurs in the day-time, and more frequent opportunities for examination are afforded, they do convince themselves of their non-existence,—and, when, as I have said before, their own reason is assisted by the more cultivated and unimpaired understanding of those around them,—when there is no art, no attempt at imposition, the whole is clearly made to appear a mere delusion, a *deceptio visus,* arising from a temporary disordered state of the animal functions, wholly independent of the persons or bodies those figures represent. But what must have been the case in other circumstances? Suppose these phantoms had only appeared in the night? — suppose the physician had affected all the arts and tricks of the designing magician, or the crafty priest — how would it have been then? — Why, precisely what we have before asserted: — they would have gone through life with a belief in the actual re-appearance of the dead, as well as the capability of communicating with the spirits of their departed friends; and thus they might have contributed their evidence to the vile impositions of those who have made a gain of the credulity of mankind, and who have, from interested motives, encouraged the fear of ghosts, the worship of demons, the belief of supernatural agency, which they could controul by their spells; of those who, like Owen Glendower, can call spirits from the vasty deep, or of the mystic masons, who pretend to show you the spirits of long departed friends. Here too we see how a Mahomet, a Swedenborg, a Jacob Behmen *, may have not

* "Behmen, or Boehm, Jacob, a shoemaker, engaged in theological controversies, was perplexed concerning many articles of faith, and prayed for divine illumination. In this state of mind he fell into a trance or ecstasy, which lasted him seven days, and afforded him an intuitive vision of God. Soon after he had a second ecstasy, was surrounded with celestial irradiation, his spirit carried to the most inward world of nature, and enabled to penetrate through external forms, lineaments, and colours of bodies, into the recess of their assembly. In a third vision, other more sublime mysteries

ON APPARITIONS.

only imposed on the world, but also on themselves, the whole farrago of their celestial communications, and converse with superior beings; and it seems to me probable, that certain professors of this art may have the power of throwing themselves into that state, in which they can bring before them those imaginary unsubstantial beings. This is no new opinion. If I remember right, it has been related of the Pythian priestess, and appears to me to be the case with the wizards of Kamschatka, and is probably the object of the whirling motion of the dervises, and of the serpent-eaters in Egypt.

---

were revealed to him — the origin of nature, formation of all things, and even divine principles and intelligent natures."

A celebrated conjuror, or mystic mason, with whom I had a conversation some years ago, told me, he could give me a receipt for a preparation of antimony, sulphur, &c., which, when burnt in a confined room, would so affect the person shut up in it, that he would fancy he saw spectres and apparitions; and that, by throwing his voice into a particular part of the room, he could make the person believe he was holding converse with spirits.

CHAP. IV.

LOCKE; HIS OPINIONS. — SHAKSPEARE — MACBETH — HAMLET. — CONCLUSION.

The common argument, by which the belief in spirits has been combated, viz. " that only one man at a time ever saw a ghost; and, therefore, the probability is, that there never was such a thing," though true, has never perhaps produced conviction, nor had the effect of removing the fears or of shaking the belief of those who have only been transiently affected with the disease, — because the mere denying of a fact, supported by supposed positive evidence, cannot produce conviction. But even this argument has been controverted; and a case has been published by Mr. Cumberland, from a paper or a memorandum, found accidentally in manuscript, one hundred years old, in which it is asserted, that some men, who lay in bed, frightened out of their wits, allowed they saw what the distempered brain of the disordered person saw. I am sorry that a story on such bad evidence should have found credit for a moment, with so respectable a writer as the author of the Observer, for the general opinion of all ages is against it; and the evidence on which this case is related, ought never to have had any weight.

It has been said by Mr. Locke, that the ideas we form of goblins and sprights have really no more to do with darkness than with light. This is certainly very just, as we have clearly seen by the foregoing relations, where the spectres appeared by day as well as by night; and yet we know they are more generally connected. This I take to be owing, not merely, as Mr. Locke says, to the association of ideas, but to the circumstance that, during the night, many sources of information are cut off, by which the true nature of these appearances might be ascertained; besides, I have reason to believe, that slight degrees of the complaint more frequently occur in the night than in the day, and that these slight and transient attacks are those which have been most commonly handed down to us.

From what I have related, it will be seen, if my theory be true, why it should happen, that only one at a time ever could see a ghost; and here we may lament, that our celebrated dramatist, whose knowledge of nature is every Englishman's boast, had not known such cases as those I have related, and their causes; he would not then, perhaps, have made his ghosts visible and audible on the stage.* Every expression, every look in Macbeth and Hamlet, is perfectly natural and consistent with men so agitated, and quite sufficient to convince us of what they see, hear, and suffer; but it must be evident, that the affection being confined solely to the individual, such objects must be seen and heard by the individual only.

"Father of all, thou gav'st not to our ken,
To view beyond the ashes of our grave."

* "Ghosts intended to haunt and affright the guilty should not appear upon the stage." Vide Walker on Italian Tragedy.

That men circumstanced as Macbeth or Hamlet, Brutus*, or Dion were, should see phantoms, and hold converse with them, appears to me perfectly natural; and, though the cases I have now related owe their origin entirely to a disordered state of bodily organs, as may be evidently inferred from the history of their rise, and the result of their cure, yet, with the knowledge we have of the effects of mind on the body, we may fairly conclude, that great mental anxiety,

* The whole story of Brutus and his evil genius rests upon Plutarch. That the phantom said, he would meet him at Philippi, may, or may not be true: that Brutus saw an apparition previously to the battle of Philippi, I believe, because I have known others, who have seen the same kind of phantom; but that the phantom told him he would meet him again at Philippi, and that he did there meet him, I do not believe. Plutarch only says, it was *reported* he did meet him there.

inordinate ambition, and guilt, may produce similar effects; nay, I am convinced, that if it were allowable for the physician to dive into the mental uneasiness of his patient, many similar facts might be added. I think, that I have known some who dared not to tell all they had seen and felt. I, some time ago, saw a man labouring under what he called a nervous complaint; I made him shrink, when I told him I knew he imagined he saw people in his room whom he did not wish to see, and others whom he knew to be dead; he rather unwillingly confessed it, when his wife had withdrawn.

I have thus endeavoured to draw the public attention to a subject not yet sufficiently investigated by the learned; and the cases which I have adduced, will, I trust, have some effect in elucidating the operations of the human mind in a state of disease, and in explaining by natural causes, what has hitherto, when believed, been attributed to supernatural agency.

THE END.

www.ingramcontent.com/pod-product-compliance
Lightning Source LLC
LaVergne TN
LVHW041310080426
835510LV00009B/945